HERRING
FISHERMEN

This book is dedicated to my three children,
Eugene F. Stephenson, John L. Stephenson and
Caroline F. Kuenstler, and my two grandchildren,
William Franklin Stephenson and
Marlon Jakob Kuenstler.

During late March or early April, as the dogwood trees bloom and a full moon shines over Carolina, millions of alewives return from the cold waters off the Canadian maritime provinces to spawn in the rivers and creeks of Eastern North Carolina. Through the years, Native Americans, English colonists and generations of fishermen from Eastern North Carolina have netted river herring in these waters.

HERRING FISHERMEN

IMAGES OF AN EASTERN NORTH CAROLINA TRADITION

FRANK STEPHENSON

Charleston   London

History
PRESS

Published by The History Press
Charleston, SC 29403
www.historypress.net

Front cover, top: "Manner of Cooking Fish," a drawing by John White of the Roanoke colony in 1585. Reprinted from *America 1585: The Complete Drawings of John White*, University of North Carolina Press, 1984. Used by permission of the publisher.
Front cover, bottom: Fishing for herring is hard, ugly and sometimes dangerous work. It takes a crew of five or six to operate a haul seine. Members of the haul seine crew at Williams Seine Fishery load the seine for another pull, or shoot, across the Meherrin River.

First published 2007

Manufactured in the United Kingdom

ISBN 978.1.59629.269.7

Library of Congress CIP data applied for.

CONTENTS

ACKNOWLEDGEMENTS

Mr. and Mrs. Dick Williams and family, Williams Seine Fishery
Mr. Dennis Layton, Parker's Ferry Fishery
Ms. Loretta Jenkins, Parker's Ferry Fishery
Ms. Barbara Nichols-Mulder, Conway, North Carolina
Mrs. Alice Nickens, Winton, North Carolina
Chowan University library staff
Mr. and Mrs. Tony Stephenson and Crew, Tunis Fishery
Mr. Terry Pratt, Merry Hill, North Carolina
Mr. David Hollowell Jr., Rocky Hock, North Carolina
Mr. Ed Hollowell, Hollowell's Fishery
Mr. and Mrs. Herbert Byrum, Byrum Brothers Fishery
Mr. Bobby Byrum, Byrum Brothers Fishery
Mr. Lee Wynns, Perry-Wynns Fish Company
Mr. Mike Perry, Perry-Wynns Fish Company
Mr. Murray L. Nixon, Murray Nixon Fishery
Mr. Ricky Nixon, Murray Nixon Fishery
Mr. and Mrs. Billy Felton, Eure, North Carolina
Mr. Bud Eure, Eure, North Carolina

Fried fresh river herring is a dish peculiar to and extremely popular in Eastern North Carolina. If the herring is not fried hard enough so that all the bones in it except the center backbone can be eaten, it is not worth the trouble to try to eat the thing. Some herring consumers prefer their fresh herring fried so hard that it resembles "cracklins" or bacon. It is then eaten as one eats corn on the cob. In fact, in some sections of Eastern North Carolina, hard-fried fresh herring is sometimes called "Roanoke River Bacon!"

INTRODUCTION

People who have lived most of their lives in Eastern North Carolina remember what the old-time mega herring runs were like. Before the fleets of European fishing trawlers parked off the North Carolina coast and scoped through the deep Atlantic waters, until the vestiges of the once great herring fishery were no longer worth the time and expense to fish. Before chemicals and other pollutants spoiled the spawning grounds in the region's rivers and streams. Before river bottomlands and tidal wetlands fell prey to development and financial bottom lines. Before dams and concrete closed a door on a migratory instinct as old as the rivers and streams themselves.

What the longtime residents of Eastern North Carolina who followed herring fishing knew is no more. The commercial herring fishing industry of Eastern North Carolina has dwindled to a paper-thin shell of its former self. The huge schools of these anadromous fish, river herring or alewife, that migrate from the cold Atlantic waters off the Canadian maritime provinces to spawn in the juniper-colored waters of Eastern North Carolina rivers and streams no longer arrive in huge numbers in the spring of the year. Residents of Eastern North Carolina could just about set their clocks by the annual migration of the millions of river herring by such sure signs as a full moon over Carolina, dogwoods in full bloom and the approach of the Easter season. The annual return of river herring to the rivers of Eastern North Carolina can be compared to the return of the buzzards to Hinckley, Ohio, and the swallows to San Juan Capistrano, California, each year.

With their dip nets, pound nets, haul seines and juniper boats, residents of Eastern North Carolina waited for the river herring to come home in March, April and May to where they had been spawned. They waited for the muddy rivers, creeks, branches and small streams to flash with white and silver. They waited for the muffled splat of herring breaking on the surface and the flapping sounds of spawning coming from the flooded lowgrounds, creek banks and riverbanks. Residents waited for the tug on a bow net, for scales dried hard and silver on the black rubber boots of pound net and haul seine crews and the smell of fresh herring and roe frying ashore in the cool March, April and May breezes.

Possibly one of the great joys of growing up in Eastern North Carolina was experiencing the annual spring herring runs and the rituals and unique culture that came with them. One such ritual involved cooking fresh-caught river herring right outside on the riverbank or creek bank. First, the herring was scaled and gutted, saving any roe. Then deep grooves were slashed about a quarter of an inch apart on both sides. The fish, breaded with flour, black pepper and salt, was then dropped into a pan of hot cooking oil and fried until one could eat the entire herring, except for the backbone. When herring is done to a point where it has turned a dark brown and is almost cremated, it is then eaten just as one plays the harmonica or eats corn on the cob. A fresh herring dinner composed of fresh fried herring, boiled potatoes, cold slaw and hush puppies is mighty fine eating. In fact, this is the dish that has made Leslie and Sally Gardner's Cypress Grill on the Roanoke River in Jamesville, North Carolina, famous. This is the very same dish that brings hundreds each spring to the Seagull Café at Perry-Wynns Fish Company on the Chowan River at Colerain, North Carolina. One cannot overlook the mighty tasty fried fresh herring plate that Mrs. Judy Williams prepares for the seine net crew at Williams Seine Fishery on the Meherrin River near Murfreesboro, North Carolina. Some people describe fresh herring dinners as a poor man's meal with a rich man's taste!

For centuries, river herring fed the eastern region of North Carolina and provided a livelihood for countless men and women employed in a colorful and thriving fishing industry. This industry was comprised mainly of a kaleidoscope of large and small herring fisheries, herring fish houses, haul seines, pound net crews and herring processing plants that included the world's largest, Perry-Wynns Fish Company which is located on the Chowan River at Colerain in Bertie County. The commercial herring fishing industry was particularly strong in Hertford, Bertie, Chowan, Northampton, Edgecombe, Halifax, Gates, Martin and other counties that bordered the Meherrin, Chowan and Roanoke Rivers in Eastern North Carolina and extended up the Nottoway, Blackwater and Meherrin Rivers in Southside Virginia where a number of herring seine fisheries were located. Herring caught in these rivers had to pass all the way through Eastern North Carolina to reach their spawning grounds in Virginia.

By 2006 the number of herring fisheries operated in Eastern North Carolina's herring spawning waters had dwindled to a very small number, occasioned by low catches and the rising costs of operating fees, licenses and fuel.

When the 2006 herring season came to a close no one was certain if there would be any more herring fishing in North Carolina waters as there was speculation that the North Carolina Marine Fisheries Commission would impose a ban on herring fishing in order to restore the stocks. The speculation became reality in late November 2006 as the North Carolina Marine Fisheries Commission imposed a ban on herring fishing in North Carolina beginning with the 2007 season. The ban marked the first time the state of North Carolina has adopted an all-out moratorium on a historically important fishery since 1991, when the state made it illegal to possess sturgeon. In all probability, the ban on herring fishing will be extended for a number of years before 2007, thus bringing an end to one of the more colorful and important chapters in North Carolina's illustrious maritime and fishing history.

Chapter One

NATIVE AMERICANS AND FISHING

When Europeans first attempted to build a settlement on what we know today as Roanoke Island, North Carolina, they were greeted by Native Americans who were probably Woodland and belonged to the Algonquian tribes. These Native Americans made their living by hunting, fishing, farming and foraging. Their principal source of meat was deer, as there were large herds roaming in Eastern North Carolina when the European settlers arrived. Deer meat was roasted over open fires and cooked in stews. Native Americans used deer for clothing, blankets and tools and utilized deer bones and antlers for needles, hoes and arrow points. Deer sinew was used for thread. The Native Americans also killed wild turkeys, rabbits, squirrels, bears and birds. They supplemented their food sources by fishing, particularly in the spring, summer and fall. The great spring herring runs were exciting times as women and children joined the men in fishing for herring. They utilized nets, hooks and traps to catch herring. Sometimes during large herring runs, Native Americans would employ barricades across streams to trap large quantities. One such place was Skinner's Gut off the Meherrin River north of Murfreesboro. When the wind blows the water out of the Meherrin River, remnants of the Native American weirs become visible at the mouth of the gut.

The Native Americans of Eastern North Carolina were as good at fishing as they were at hunting. The many large rivers and sounds of Eastern North Carolina provided large quantities of fish for them. With such a vast food supply at hand, the Native Americans must not have been in the region long before they began using different methods to take fish in large quantities. The huge spring runs of herring may have been one of their easier preys.

Several archaeological studies have shown that Native Americans residing along or near the Chowan and Roanoke Rivers were adept at fishing. It appears that they took fish in traps and utilized spears, arrows and hooks. Native American shell mounds located on the Chowan and Roanoke Rivers have yielded large quantities of fish bones, including those of herring. One such site in Hertford County, near the Chowan River, produced quantities of herring, shad and garfish bones. Garfish were usually taken by some kind of trap rather than by a hook. Bonefish hooks have also been found along the Chowan and Cashie Rivers along with bones of the big channel catfish. The first European settlers found that at times the Native Americans were taking fish in large quantities. Hooks and lines were employed in general use and some fish were shot with bows and arrows. In dry seasons when streams would dry up into pools, fish were sometimes poisoned with a plant extract that was not lethal to humans.

At night, the Tuscaroras of Eastern North Carolina sometimes built fires on the riverbanks or creekbanks to attract fish. The fish were then harvested by reed baskets or shot with arrows. Native Americans who lived closer to larger bodies of water would build fires in or hold torches from canoes to fish at night. When the fish were attracted to the firelight, young men took great sport in seeing how many fish each could harpoon. Hooks, lines, nets and weirs were all utilized in Eastern North Carolina by Native Americans for fishing.

Weirs were used extensively by Native Americans in Eastern North Carolina to fish for river herring. The weirs would almost totally block up a stream or creek, leaving only a small, restricted passage for herring and shad to enter and at the same time preventing their escape. River herring were caught in great numbers by Native Americans in Eastern North Carolina. Large quantities of the river herring were preserved by air drying in the sun or roasting over a smoldering fire.

The large sturgeon found in numbers in the rivers of Eastern North Carolina did not escape the attention of Native American fishermen. Native Americans employed different methods to capture large sturgeon, including harpooning, lassoing and driving them in shallow pools of water and literally riding them until they were tired and could be tossed up on shore. The Native Americans roasted or broiled sturgeon meat but would not eat the sturgeon roe for fear that it would poison them. The late Roger Cullifer, who operated a small country living museum at Mount Gould on the Chowan River in Bertie County, North Carolina, stated that when he was a young boy in the early 1900s, sturgeon were often caught in the large haul seines. The sturgeon meat was used, but the black sturgeon roe was always buried because it was lethal to dogs, cats, chickens and other small animals or fowl that might eat it.

Eastern North Carolina is laced with an elaborate system of rivers and creeks like the Chowan and Meherrin Rivers pictured here. Native Americans made their homes near these rivers primarily for transportation and the plentiful supply of fish such as river herring. Most of the rivers in Eastern North Carolina had herring runs, but the Chowan, Meherrin and Roanoke Rivers were prime spawning grounds.

INDIAN VILLAGE OF SECOTON (no. 38A, cf. pl. 135)

Fishing on Eastern North Carolina rivers and creeks represented a large part of Native Americans' search for food. John White of the Roanoke Island colony drew this view of Native Americans fishing. The huge herring runs in the spring were important to Native Americans in their quest for food. *Reprinted from* America 1585: The Complete Drawings Of John White. *Copyright 1984 by the University of North Carolina Press. Used by permission of the publisher.*

Opposite: Eastern North Carolina was home to Native American tribes and their villages were numerous and scattered about the region. One such village, Secoton, is shown here in one of John White's drawings from the Roanoke Island colony. *Reprinted from* America 1585: The Complete Drawings Of John White. *Copyright 1984 by the University of North Carolina Press. Used by permission of the publisher.*

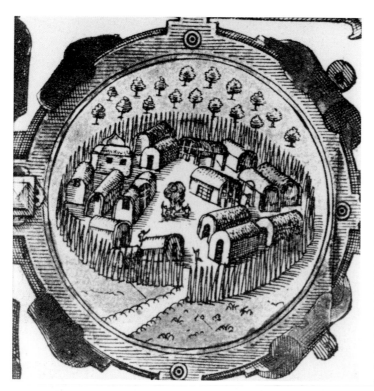

The Meherrin town, Ramushouuong, near Parker's Ferry on the Meherrin River in Hertford County bore strong resemblance to this engraving in the 1606 Mercator-Hondius Map. *Frank Stephenson Photo Archives.*

The Meherrin were one of many Native American tribes that enjoyed huge spring runs of herring. Their village, Ramushouuong, was located on the Meherrin River in Hertford County at Parker's Ferry where the Chowan and Meherrin Rivers meet. This state historical maker is located on U.S. 158, approximately one mile west of Winton, North Carolina.

Right: When huge spring runs of herring appeared, Native Americans used weirs and other methods to block up small streams or guts to trap large quantities of fish. Skinner's, a gut off the Meherrin River, was blocked by Native Americans. Evidence of this can be seen when the wind blows the water out and exposes the remains of weirs at the entrance to the gut.

Below: The Potecasi Creek was also blocked by Native Americans during spring herring runs. This gut is actually man-made and is thought to have been dug by Native Americans, or perhaps slaves.

Many of the streams in Eastern North Carolina, such as the Potecasi Creek, remain in a semi-wild or wild state and have been major spawning grounds for river herring.

The Somerton Creek in Gates County has also been a valuable herring spawning ground. This creek is a tributary of the Chowan River.

Chapter Two

HAUL SEINES, DRAG SEINES AND PULL SEINES

One of the more popular methods used in commercial herring fishing in colonial times and many years thereafter was the haul seine, which is sometimes called the drag or pull seine. The river seine was first introduced to the herring spawning waters of North Carolina in the 1740s by John Campbell, a British navy captain. Campbell sought his fortune in the New World and purchased eight hundred acres of land at Colerain in Bertie County along the Chowan River. It was at Colerain where John Campbell placed in operation the first haul seine in North Carolina. It did not take long for this method of herring fishing to become popular. Numerous herring fishing seines large and small sprung up along the Chowan and other rivers, streams and sounds in Eastern North Carolina, as river herring would arrive in huge numbers in these waters. Farmers purchased herring by the cartload from nearby seine fisheries to salt down in barrels, as salt herring were a main part of their diet along with beans, potatoes and corn pone.

The huge haul seine located in Hertford County at Petty Shore was an example of one of the great seines that operated on the Chowan River and other large bodies of water in the region. Then there were the scores of smaller seines that operated on the upper reaches of the Chowan River, the Meherrin River—both in North Carolina and Virginia—and Nottoway and Blackwater Rivers in southern Virginia. Herring that were caught in the aforementioned Virginia locations had reached their spawning grounds via the Chowan River. In 1814, Joseph F. Dickins was operating a small "half-moon" seine fishery in Gates County on the Chowan River above Winton. In the late 1800s and early 1900s there was a haul seine operating at Maney's on the Hertford County side of the Chowan River just below the North Carolina–Virginia line where the Nottoway and Blackwater Rivers merge to form the Chowan River in North Carolina. The late Dillard Riddick, who lived at Maney's or Riddicksville, told me that there was a small herring seine operating in Gates County across from Maney's Fishery. While the Blackwater River was one of the herring spawning grounds, in neighboring Virginia there were not a large number of haul seines operating on it primarily because of its bank configuration. There were, however, several small seines operating in the Joyner's Bridge area of the Blackwater River north of Franklin, Virginia. These were operated by Garnett Whitley, Roland Whitley and John Vaughan, respectively.

Haul seining on the Nottoway River above the Chowan River was much different than on the Blackwater River. On the edge of Virginia, at Battle's Beach on the Nottoway

River, herring haul seines were operated there for many years. John Reese, Paul Jenkins and Ralph Stradley were among the last to operate a seine at Battle's Beach. The Tyler Edwards family operated a herring seine on the Nottoway River for over fifty years near Monroe Bridge. Some of the seine masters at the Tyler Edwards Fishery were Taylor Harcum, Tyler Edwards, Clyde Edwards, Carlyle Edwards and John Moody. When I was a boy, I accompanied my grandfather, Sam Bishop of Sunbeam, Virginia, on several trips to the Tyler Edwards Fishery. Cotton's Seine Fishery, operated by seine masters Pat, Dellie and Will Cotton, was located not far upstream from the Tyler Edwards Fishery on the Nottoway River and Pope's Seine Fishery. Dewey Howell and his brother Edward operated a small haul seine on the Nottoway River at Point Beach. There had been a herring fishery located at Cypress Bridge on the Nottoway River, but the flood of 1918 destroyed it. In later years Willie Shaw operated a herring seine at Cypress Bridge on the Handsom side of the Nottoway River. In the Delaware area of the Nottoway River, Hersey Underwood had a haul seine that could be rented by the day. There were haul seines located above the Delaware area and these included Vick's Seine Beach, operated by Joe Vick and Roger Whitfield's Seine Beach. Many of the herring caught at haul seines operating on the Blackwater and Nottoway Rivers in lower Virginia were sold to Perry-Wynns Fish Company in Colerain, North Carolina.

In 1815, William P. Little was operating a small seine fishery at the site we know today as Parker's Ferry in Hertford County on the Meherrin River below Murfreesboro. The Parker's Ferry site was the location of numerous herring seines, including the Gary Parker Fishery, the Revelle Fishery, the Cephus Futrell Fishery and others. The Meherrin River in North Carolina was the location of numerous small haul seines through the years, particularly between Parker's Ferry and Murfreesboro. In fact, the last operating commercial haul seine in North Carolina, Williams Seine Fishery, is located on the Meherrin River about a mile below Murfreesboro. In 1967 Calvin Pearce and Bob Shaver opened a small haul seine between Williams Fishery and Murfreesboro on the Meherrin River. There were small haul seines located on the Meherrin River between Murfreesboro and the Virginia state line, including Eugene Reid's Fishery, the Princeton Fishery, Cooper's Fishery and Brett's Fishery. Herring that came up the Meherrin River to spawn did not stop at the Virginia–North Carolina state line. There was some commercial herring fishing on the Meherrin River from the state line all the way to Emporia and Stony Creek, Virginia, where the Prince family operated a small herring seine.

Haul seining is a way of life and culture that is all but gone. If it were not for the Williams family, who have operated North Carolina's last haul, Williams Seine Fishery, on the Meherrin River near Murfreesboro, there would be no more links to the great era of haul seining in North Carolina. We can fondly recall such giant haul seines as Capehart's Fishery, Sutton's Fishery, Eden House Fishery, Holly's Fishery, Poole's Fishery and others, or we can remember the small seines such as Williams Fishery.

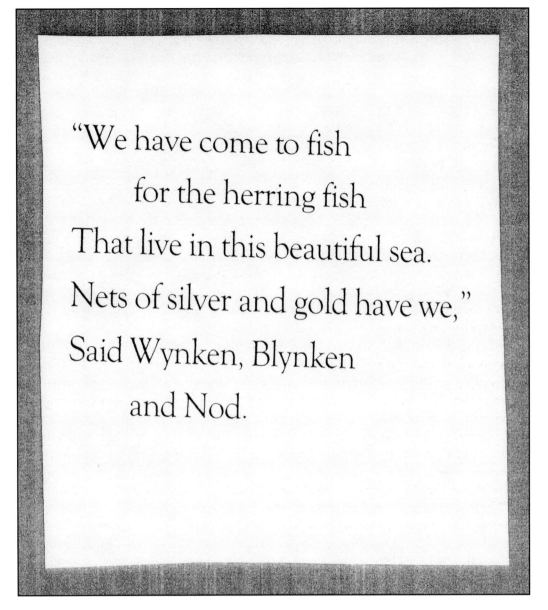

"We have come to fish
    for the herring fish
That live in this beautiful sea.
Nets of silver and gold have we,"
Said Wynken, Blynken
    and Nod.

From the book *Wynken, Blynken and Nod. Courtesy of Scholastic Publications, Inc., New York, New York.*

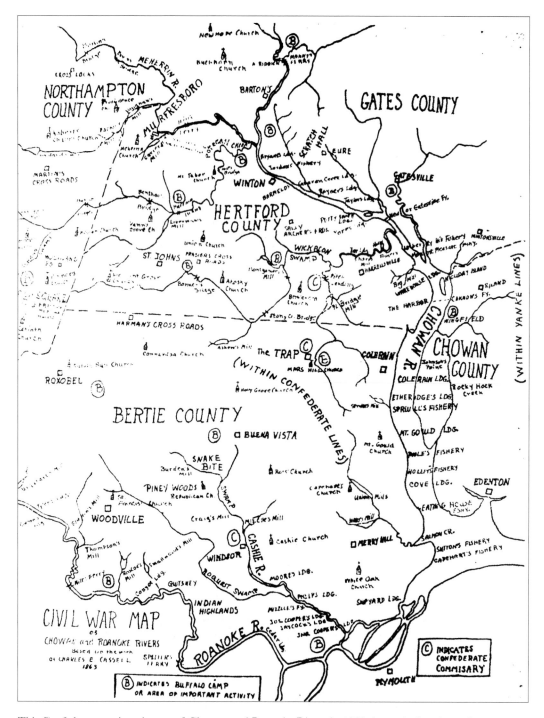

This Confederate engineer's map of Chowan and Roanoke Rivers in 1863 shows the locations of a number of herring fisheries. *Courtesy North Carolina Department of Cultural Resources.*

Drawing of the Belvidere Fishery in the Albemarle from *Harper's New Monthly Magazine*, March 1857. *Courtesy North Carolina Department of Cultural Resources.*

Taking the herring seine out in the Edenton region. From *Harper's New Monthly Magazine*, March 1857. *Courtesy North Carolina Department of Cultural Resources.*

HAULING THE SEINE.

Hauling the seine or bringing it in once it has been strung out in the Edenton area. From *Harper's Weekly*, March 15, 1862. *Courtesy North Carolina Department of Cultural Resources.*

A night haul in the Edenton area. From *Harper's New Monthly Magazine*, March 1857. *Courtesy North Carolina Department of Cultural Resources.*

Heading herring in the Albemarle area. From *Harper's New Monthly Magazine*, March 1857. *Courtesy North Carolina Department of Cultural Resources.*

Haul seine fishing at Sutton Beach on the Albemarle Sound in the late 1800s. *Courtesy North Carolina Department of Cultural Resources.*

Landing herring at Capehart's Fishery at Avoca in Bertie County in the 1880s. *Frank Stephenson Photo Archives.*

Tarring the seine in Perquimans County in the late 1800s. *Courtesy North Carolina Department of Cultural Resources.*

Removing the roe from sturgeon caught at Capehart's Fishery in the late 1800s. *Frank Stephenson Photo Archives*.

Steam seine boat at Capehart's Fishery in 1884. *Courtesy North Carolina Department of Cultural Resources.*

Capehart's Fishery in 1884. *Courtesy North Carolina Department of Cultural Resources.*

Capehart's Fishery in 1903. *Courtesy North Carolina Department of Cultural Resources.*

Steam seine boat at Capehart's Fishery in 1884. *Courtesy North Carolina Department of Cultural Resources.*

Left: Herring smoker, Eden Point, Edenton, May 1949. *Courtesy North Carolina Department of Cultural Resources.*

Below: Wooden barrels used to salt herring at Eden Point, Edenton, May 1949. *Courtesy North Carolina Department of Cultural Resources.*

Opposite above: Undated photograph of a haul seine village in the Albemarle region of North Carolina. *Frank Stephenson Photo Archives.*

Opposite below: Cutting herring in 1940 at Eden Point, Edenton. *Courtesy North Carolina Department of Cultural Resources.*

Left: The process of laying out the haul seine across the river is sometimes called "shooting the seine." Here crew members shoot the seine near Plymouth on the Roanoke River in May 1939. *Courtesy North Carolina Department of Cultural Resources.*

Below: Herring fishing at Jamesville on the Roanoke River in May 1939. *Courtesy North Carolina Department of Cultural Resources.*

Herring fishing at Jamesville on the
Roanoke River in May 1939. *Courtesy
North Carolina Department of Cultural
Resources.*

Herring fishing seine house at Plymouth on
the Roanoke River in May 1939. *Courtesy North
Carolina Department of Cultural Resources.*

Left: Salting fresh-cut herring at Jamesville on the Roanoke River in May 1939. *Courtesy North Carolina Department of Cultural Resources.*

Below: Herring seine fishing at Plymouth on the Roanoke River in May 1939. *Courtesy North Carolina Department of Cultural Resources.*

Maddrey's Herring Fishery on the north side of the Meherrin River in 1905. In 1825, Murfreesboro diarist Dr. Thomas O'Dwyer mentioned a seine at this site and how plentiful the herring had been that season. Dr. O'Dwyer mentioned other nearby herring seines in his diary and it appears that he was part owner of one of the seines. *Frank Stephenson Photo Archives.*

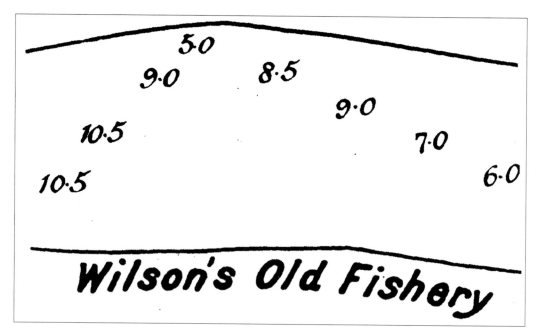

This 1885 map of the Meherrin River shows the location of Wilson's Old Fishery about four miles south of Murfreesboro. *Frank Stephenson Photo Archives*.

Wilson's Old Fishery stood about four miles south of Murfreesboro on the south side of the Meherrin River. It was one of a number of small herring seines that dotted the banks of the Meherrin River for many years. *Frank Stephenson Photo Archives*.

11.5

15.5 15.5
16.7
14.5
10.5 14.0 16.0 11.5

13.0
12.0
9.7
7.5

Mud Hole Fishery

3.0
9.3
13.5
14.0
14.0

This 1885 map of the Meherrin River shows the location of Mud Hole Fishery about five miles south of Murfreesboro on the north side of the Meherrin River. In 1919, when my father Frank Stephenson Sr. was ten years old, he and his brother Lee Stephenson were at the seine when a sturgeon weighing 340 pounds was caught in one of the hauls. According to my father, the sturgeon was about ten feet long and it took about three hours to land. Cade Bynum was foreman of Mud Hole Fishery the day the big sturgeon was caught. *Frank Stephenson Photo Archives*.

Ben Whitley of Murfreesboro owned and operated Mud Hole Seine Fishery for about fifteen years. He was at the seine the day the big fish was caught. *Photo courtesy of Sam Whitley, son of Ben Whitley.*

1920s view Paul Jordan's Seine Fishery that was located on the Meherrin River near Como. This image shows the haul seine crew loading the seine for another shoot across the Meherrin River. *Frank Stephenson Photo Archives.*

1920s view of Paul Jordan's Seine Fishery that was located on the Meherrin River near Como. This image shows the haul seine crew using the windlass to slowly bring the seine to shore. *Frank Stephenson Photo Archives.*

1920s view of Paul Jordan's Seine Fishery that was located on the Meherrin River near Como. Here, the haul seine crew cleans out the seine prior to another haul. *Frank Stephenson Photo Archives*.

1965 view of some of the boats used at Paul Jordan's Seine Fishery that was located on the Meherrin River near Como.

This is an undated poster advertising salt or corned herring for sale at the Mount Gallant Seine Fishery that was located at Chowan Beach on the Chowan River about one mile above Winton. *Frank Stephenson Photo Archives.*

The Mount Gallant Fishery was operated by Eli Reid of Winton and Charles L. Revelle Sr., shown here. Mr. Revelle was a businessman from Murfreesboro and he and Mr. Reid operated Mount Gallant Fishery for about ten years. *Frank Stephenson Photo Archives*.

In addition to co-owning Mount Gallant Fishery with Charles L. Revelle Sr., Eli Reid developed and operated Chowan Beach Amusement Park from 1926 to 1967. *Frank Stephenson Photo Archives*.

Left: Hundreds of freshly caught herring at Mount Gallant Seine Fishery await pickup and processing in this early 1930s photo. *Frank Stephenson Photo Archives.*

Below: Members of the 1941 Mount Gallant herring seine crew work the seine toward shore where the fish will be dumped and sorted. *Photograph by Joel C. Holland.*

Right: John Askew of Winton, North Carolina, was seine master for many years at the Mount Gallant Herring Fishery at Chowan Beach. He would implore his twenty-man crew to perform their tasks by employing a chant similar to those used at sea. *1941 photograph by Joel C. Holland.*

Below: The Chowan Beach waterfront awash in freshly caught herring at Mount Gallant Seine Fishery. *1941 photograph by Joel C. Holland.*

Left: As seen in this 1941 photograph, the herring seine at Mount Gallant Seine Fishery was no small operation in either manpower or technology. The herring seine itself was so long and large that it required several boats with inboard motors to pull the heavily laden seine across the Chowan River. *1941 photograph by Joel C. Holland.*

Below: The Mount Gallant Herring Fishery crew lands another haul of herring in the early 1930s. *Frank Stephenson Photo Archives.*

Opposite above: The herring haul seine crew rolls hundreds of freshly caught herring onto the beach at Mount Gallant Fishery in the 1930s. *Frank Stephenson Photo Archives.*

Opposite below: This 1941 photograph provides a glimpse inside the herring processing house at Mount Gallant Fishery. In later years, this building was converted into a beachfront dance hall as part of the Chowan Beach Amusement Park. *1941 photograph by Joel C. Holland.*

Herring cutters at work in the processing house at Mount Gallant Fishery. *1941 photograph by Joel C. Holland.*

Vats of freshly caught and salted river herring in the processing house at Mount Gallant Fishery. *1941 photograph by Joel C. Holland.*

Sign for Williams Seine Fishery, located on the Meherrin River about two miles south of Murfreesboro. There has been a haul seine operating at this location for over one hundred years. At the close of the 2006 herring fishing season, Williams Seine Fishery was the last operating haul seine in North Carolina. Since the early 1990s, the seine fishery has been operated by Mr. and Mrs. Dick Willams and family.

Riverfront view of Williams Seine Fishery.

The haul seine at Williams Seine Fishery is stretched across the Meherrin River before the crew begins the process of pulling, or hauling, the net to shore to process the catch.

Seine Master Dick Williams and his wife, Judy, have operated Williams Seine Fishery for over fifteen years and have preserved an excellent example of this unique way of life and culture in North Carolina. The operation of North Carolina's last haul seine is a family affair by these wonderful and gracious people. Seine Master and Mrs. Williams are assisted in this labor-intensive herring fishing operation by their extended family, consisting of children, grandchildren, friends, neighbors and anyone else who is willing to strap on a pair of waders, get their hands wet and be a part of something that is truly very special.

Seine Master Louis Griffith holds up a poisonous snake he killed at his seine fishery, which he operated for about fifty years. *Courtesy Mrs. Sarah Griffith Fentress.*

Seine Master Eugene Reid of Murfreesboro operated Griffith's Seine Fishery for about ten years. Later he operated a small herring seine on the Meherrin River above Murfreesboro for five years. *Courtesy the Eugene Reid Family.*

Right: Seine Master George Williams, brother of Seine Master Dick Williams, operated Williams Seine Fishery in the 1970s and 1980s.

Below: It was always a lot of fun to purchase a mess of herring at Griffith's Seine Fishery. The herring were usually strung on a piece of baling wire for easy transport home. *1950s photograph by Roy Johnson.*

Members of the haul seine crew at Williams Seine Fishery load the seine for another shoot across the Meherrin River.

Fishing for herring is hard, ugly and sometimes dangerous work. It takes a crew of five to six to operate a haul seine. Members of the crew at Williams Seine Fishery load the seine for another pull, or shoot, across the Meherrin River.

Haul seiners at Williams Seine Fishery load the seine for another haul, or shoot, across the Meherrin River. The net is strung out across the river for a short period of time and then pulled or hauled to the shore for dumping the catch, which can be small in number or several thousand when the herring are running well.

Haul seiners at Williams Seine Fishery have loaded the seine for another shoot across the Meherrin River.

Haul seiners at Williams Seine Fishery lay out or shoot the seine across the Meherrin River.

The Williams Seine Fishery crew shoot the seine across the Meherrin River.

Haul seiners at Williams Seine Fishery slowly work the seine along the shore toward the fish box for dumping the catch.

Haul seiners eventually dump the catch in the fish box.

Haul seiners at Williams Seine Fishery slowly work the seine toward the fish box for dumping.

Haul seiners at Williams Seine Fishery are careful to keep the lead line on the river bottom to prevent fish from escaping beneath the seine net.

Men and women at Williams Seine Fishery work side by side.

Dumping the seine to see what has been caught is the fun part of haul seining at Williams Seine Fishery.

Left: Following a shoot across the Meherrin River, members of the Williams Seine Fishery crew dump the seine.

Below: The fun of haul seining is finally seeing what has been caught. Here, members of the Williams Seine Fishery crew dump the catch in the fish box.

Haul seiners at Williams Seine Fishery dump the seine following another pull across the Meherrin River.

Removing the catch from the seine following another haul across the Meherrin River at Williams Seine Fishery.

Members of the haul seine crew at Williams Seine Fishery collect the catch following another shoot across the Meherrin River.

Larry Vick, one of the haul seiners at Williams Seine Fishery, repairs the seine net.

Mrs. Frances Byrum and Mrs. Judy Williams clean herring at Williams Seine Fishery.

Mrs. Judy Williams, chief cook at Williams
Seine Fishery, cooks up another delicious
batch of fried fresh herring to feed a bunch of
hungry haul seiners and anyone else who might
be on hand at lunchtime. There are rarely any
leftovers!

Haul seiner and cook Richard Harrell cooks another
batch of tasty fried fresh herring at Williams Seine
Fishery.

Seine Master Dick Williams and son, Barry, are shown here repairing the seine net. From time to time holes are torn by snags in the Meherrin River.

Members of the Williams Seine Fishery crew watch as fellow haul seiner Tim Byrum holds a twenty-five pound rockfish that was caught in the seine. The huge fish was returned to the waters of the Meherrin River without harm.

Williams Seine Fishery crew members Barry Williams and Ryan Williams enjoy a break at the fishery in April 2006. The two haul seiners are the son and grandson of Seine Master and Mrs. Dick Williams.

Seine Master Eugene Reid operated this herring seine at Sandy Shores on the Meherrin River just above Murfreesboro for about five years. *Frank Stephenson Photo Archives*.

Seine Master Eugene Reid and his haul seine crew dump the seine in the fish box at the herring seine fishery that he operated at Sandy Shores on the Meherrin River just above Murfreesboro. *Frank Stephenson Photo Archives*.

Chapter Three

POUND OR DUTCH NETS

Prior to 1869, the main method of commercial herring fishing in Eastern North Carolina's herring spawning grounds was the employment of huge haul or drag seines. Many of these seines averaged from 2,000 to 2,700 yards in length and dragged the bottoms of large areas of water. In the 1890s and early 1900s there were a number of large haul seines in operation at such places as Drummond's Point, Bluff Point, Greenfield, Sandy Point, Avoca and other points on the Chowan and Roanoke Rivers and the Albemarle Sound. These giant seines needed large crews to operate and often required twenty to thirty men, along with a number of women, who were mainly employed as herring cutters, roe pickers and packers. In stark contrast to the large expense of operating a giant haul seine, a herring fisherman who utilized pound or Dutch nets could work twenty to thirty of them with a crew of four to five men, thus reducing the costs of operation. Twenty- to thirty-pound nets could provide large catches of herring in good seasons and made the shift from large haul seines to pound nets popular among herring fishermen. The word "pound" refers to the way the fish are caught. Fish follow a shore line to the main net where they enter an impoundment area and are trapped with no way out.

This brings us to the question of when pound net fishing was introduced to North Carolina and who was responsible. The man responsible for introducing pound nets to North Carolina is John Penrose Hettrick, who was a Dutchman from Selensgrove, Pennsylvania. John Penrose Hettrick and his younger brother, William, first began their fishing careers on the Great Lakes at Erie and Huron, Erie County, Ohio, using a revolutionary type of net called a Dutch net. During the Civil War, John Penrose Hettrick came to the Albemarle region of North Carolina as a Union soldier. Interested in fishing, he inquired about fishing possibilities in this region of North Carolina and was informed that thousands of herring were caught in the spring in single hauls by seines—the only method used at that time. John Penrose Hettrick decided that this was the place for him to come after the war and brought with him his new type of net. So in 1869, John Penrose Hettrick came south with fishing equipment and settled on the Albemarle Sound near Edenton, North Carolina. He established a fishery at Sandy Point and introduced pound or Dutch nets to North Carolina for the first time by setting some in the Albemarle Sound. In a short time, John Penrose Hettrick had moved his family from Pennsylvania to Edenton, purchased considerable other property and extensively fished the waters of Albemarle Sound for herring. In 1878,

William H. Hettrick joined his brother, John, in Edenton and both enjoyed long and prosperous herring fishing careers there.

It did not take long for pound nets to catch on in North Carolina herring fishing waters and as more were utilized, many of the huge haul seines went out of business. At one time there were more than five thousand pound nets setting in the Croatan and Albemarle Sounds and the Chowan River region, extending from Oregon Inlet to Winton on the Chowan River—a distance of about one hundred miles.

The introduction of pound net fishing in Eastern North Carolina herring spawning waters in 1869 was the catalyst for the development of a huge commercial fishing industry in Eastern North Carolina that fostered the growth and development of several large herring fisheries and herring processing companies, particularly along the Chowan River. The largest of these herring fisheries and herring processing plants was Perry-Wynns Fish Company located on the Chowan River at Colerain. Perry-Wynns Fish Company, organized in 1953 by Leo Wynns and L. D. Perry, grew into the world's largest herring processing facility and Colerain became known as the herring capital of the world.

In 1966, Perry-Wynns Fish Company expanded its herring processing capacity by purchasing the Cannon's Ferry operation of Standard Products Company of White Stone, Virginia. This meant that the company was expanding across the Chowan River. This purchase at Cannon's Ferry included the fish processing plant, the new canning plant, the fish meal plant and all machinery and equipment, including trucks and boats. Perry-Wynns Fish Company produced a number of products through the years. Included in these were salt fish in plastic bags; tubs, tins, pails and jars with herring fillets and vinegar-cured herring; canned herring roe and river herring. During the height of Perry-Wynns Fish Company, it employed over two hundred seasonal and permanent workers, such as herring cutters, roe pickers and packers who utilized more than one million pounds of salt and 25,000 gallons of vinegar yearly.

In September 2003, a tragedy beyond belief struck Perry-Wynns Fish Company when Hurricane Isabel roared up the Chowan River and destroyed nine of the company's eleven buildings, putting it out of business. Today, Perry-Wynns Fish Company is recovering and back in business, proudly selling fish products that made the company world famous.

While Perry-Wynns Fish Company is located on the west bank of the Chowan River in Bertie County, Rocky Hock, a neighborly farming and fishing community, is located a little upstream on the opposite side of the river. Here, generations of old families such as the Nixons, Laytons, Bunches, Byrums, Basses, Feltons, Peeles, Tynches, Lanes and Learys have farmed and fished for herring using pound nets. This area is also home to a large national import-export wholesale and retail fishing operation, Murrary Nixon's Fishery. Murray Nixon began his fishery by selling herring out of the back of a pickup truck part-time in the late 1950s. Murray Nixon's part-time business soon turned into a full-time operation with over seventy employees and a solid reputation up and down the East Coast.

John P. Hettrick, along with his brother William, is credited with introducing pound nets to North Carolina. The Hettrick brothers were Dutchmen from Selensgrove, Pennsylvania, who began their fishing careers on the Great Lakes at Erie and Huron, Erie County, Ohio, using a revolutionary type of net called the Dutch or pound net. The older Hettrick brother, John, came to the Albemarle region of North Carolina as a Union soldier during the Civil War. He soon discovered the great opportunities for commercial fishing in the region and returned in 1869 with his Dutch or pound nets. *Courtesy North Carolina Department of Cultural Resources*.

In 1878 William H. Hettrick joined his brother, John, in Edenton where both enjoyed long and prosperous herring fishing careers. *Courtesy North Carolina Department of Cultural Resources*.

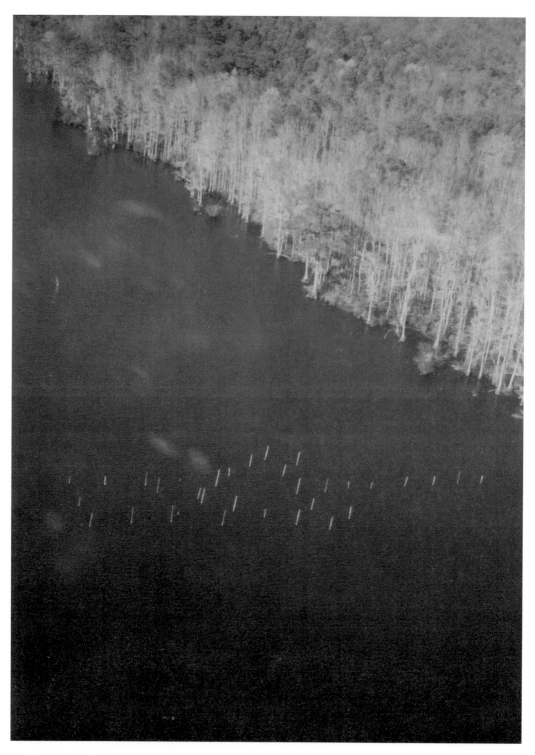

Aerial view of a Chowan River pound or Dutch net. At the height of the great herring runs, there were over a thousand pound nets on the Chowan River. *Photograph by Frank Stephenson with plane service provided and piloted by Dr. J.A. Fleetwood Jr., of Conway, North Carolina.*

This Parker's Ferry Fishery sign, painted by Dennis Layton, stood on U.S. 258 south of Como. Parker's Ferry Fishery was established in 1942 by Raymond Layton and Richard Lee Williams of Chowan County, North Carolina. The fishery was located about eight miles south of Murfreesboro on the Meherrin River at Parker's Ferry and stood there until 1999 when Hurricane Floyd destroyed it.

Dennis and Loretta Layton operated Parker's Ferry Fishery seasonally for about ten years. Their principal source of herring was pound nets set on the Meherrin and Chowan Rivers. Fishing for herring with pound nets is not for the lazy or fainthearted. It is hard, ugly, cold, nasty and dangerous work. Four members of Dennis Layton's family have been lost to the Chowan and Meherrin Rivers through herring fishing.

Parker's Ferry Fishery as it appeared in the 1970s. The main fish house structure on the right side was moved from the Black Rock Fishery on the Chowan River in the 1950s by Dennis Layton's father. This view shows a conveyor used to load large quantities of herring into tractor-trailers and dump trucks.

Parker's Ferry Fishery as it appeared from the Meherrin River in the 1970s. Huge quantities of river herring were landed here.

Another view of the Black Rock fish house that was moved to Parker's Ferry Fishery in the 1950s.

One of the river scenes that was painted at Parker's Ferry Fishery by Dennis Layton.

Members of the Parker's Ferry Fishery pound net crew fish one of their pound nets on the Chowan River.

Pound netters from Parker's Ferry Fishery fish one of their pound nets on the Chowan River.

Dennis and Loretta Layton of Parker's Ferry Fishery fish one of their pound nets on the Meherrin River.

Dennis and Loretta Layton of Parker's Ferry Fishery fish one of their pound nets on the Chowan River.

Right and below: Loretta Layton of Parker's Ferry Fishery fishes a pound net on the Chowan River. She can attest that it is hard work.

Dennis Layton of Parker's Ferry Fishery rolls the catch from a pound net into his boat on the Meherrin River.

Tractor-trailer load of freshly caught herring at Parker's Ferry Fishery headed to a processing plant in Norfolk, Virginia, in 1976.

Pile driver that Dennis Layton of Parker's Ferry Fishery used to drive pound net stakes into river bottoms. Some of the newly cut pound net stakes can be seen on the deck of the pile driver.

Dennis Layton at Parker's Ferry Fishery knew a number of ways to process herring. This is a string of his air-dried herring. The freshly caught herring are cleaned and briefly dipped into salt water and then hung out to dry.

Parker's Ferry, which crosses the Meherrin River in Hertford County, is one of three remaining river ferries operating in North Carolina today. The other two operate in Bertie and Bladen Counties.

Loretta Layton of Parker's Ferry Fishery sorts out the catch following a trip to the pound nets on the Meherrin and Chowan Rivers.

Dennis Layton of Parker's Ferry Fishery weighs part of the catch from a trip to the pound nets.

Dennis and Loretta Layton's Throw Down at Parker's Ferry Fishery.

Right: In 1989, Tony Stephenson of Winton—along with Lynn Harrell, Olin Romines and Robert Pearson—opened a small pound net fishery at Tuscarora or Barfields on the Chowan River between Winton and Tunis. This is one of their fish house signs.

Below: Tony Stephenson's Fishery, which was located at Tuscarora or Barfields on the Chowan River. In earlier times, Barfields was the site of a ferry crossing the Chowan River to Gates County and several large herring haul seines. Tony Stephenson and his pound net crew operated this fishery for five years until 1994, when he moved his operation to Tunis Fishery, which is located on the Chowan River at Tunis.

Tony Stephenson, who operated his small pound net fishery at Tuscarora or Barfields for five years until 1994.

Left: For many years, Tunis, North Carolina had been a railroad and fishing village overlooking the Chowan River in Hertford County. Here, an Atlantic Coast Line stream engine taking on water at Tunis in the winter of 1936. By 1994, when Tony Stephenson moved his herring fishing operation to Tunis, the railroad had ceased operation. *Courtesy Mrs. S. Eure, Eure, North Carolina.*

Opposite above: Jobe Williams, Brantley Jeffries and Leroy Eure fishing pound nets on the Chowan River off Tunis in the late 1950s. *Frank Stephenson Photo Archives.*

Opposite below: This May 5, 1955 photo shows Tunis pound net fishermen Tas Mattherson, Brantley Jefferies, Jobe Williams and Walter Jefferies unloading herring at Parrish's fish house in Tunis. *Courtesy the* Roanoke-Chowan News-Herald, *Ahoskie, North Carolina.*

Another view of the May 5, 1955 photo showing Tas Mattherson, Brantley Jefferies, Jobe Williams and Walter Jefferies unloading herring at Parrish's Fish House at Tunis. *Courtesy the* Roanoke-Chowan News-Herald, *Ahoskie, North Carolina.*

This May 5, 1955 photo shows Lindsay Parrish Jr., a Chowan River pound net fisherman, at his fish house at Tunis. *Courtesy the* Roanoke-Chowan News-Herald, *Ahoskie, North Carolina.*

This is a 1949 view of Peter Griffith's fish house (foreground) and several homes that stood on the edge of the Chowan River on the north side of the railroad tracks at Tunis. *Courtesy North Carolina Department of Cultural Resources.*

1950s view Peter Griffith's fish house on the edge of the Chowan River. Peter Griffith (center) spent most of his life as a fisherman on the Chowan River. At one time he also had a small fish house on the east side of the Chowan River in Gates County across from Tunis. His brother, Louis, operated the Williams Fishery haul seine on the Meherrin River for over fifty years. *Frank Stephenson Photo Archives.*

Left: This late 1940s view of Peter Griffith's fish house at Tunis shows Peter Griffith (second from right) with his daughter, Thelma Shaver (third from right), and her husband, Bob Shaver (far right). The woman on the left is unidentified. Bob Shaver worked with his father-in-law in both Griffith's fish house and Tunis Fishery. In the 1960s, Bob Shaver teamed with Calvin Pearce of Murfreesboro to operate a small herring seine fishery about two miles south of Murfreesboro on the Meherrin River. *Frank Stephenson Photo Archives.*

Below: This is an odd little ditty that appeared in the May 4, 1944 issue of the *Roanoke-Chowan News-Herald. Frank Stephenson Photo Archives.*

Fishing is a great business down on the Chowan River these days. In one section one day last week everywhere I went they were cutting and salting away fish. One lady of the house came out to meet me with a knife in one hand and a herring in the other.

In May 1944, Frank Stephenson Sr. (left) and his uncle, Peter B. Griffith, cook herring on the riverbank at Griffith's herring fishery at Tunis on the Chowan River. *Frank Stephenson Photo Archives*.

Left: This is a 1980s sign for Tunis Fishery, which is located at Tunis on the Chowan River in Hertford County.

Below: This is a 1980s view of Tunis Fishery. A number of fishermen have operated Tunis Fishery since it was built in the 1940s, including Peter Griffith, Bob Shaver, Walter Jefferies, Brantley Jefferies, Victor Perry and Tony Stephenson, who remodeled it as it stands today.

Brantley Jefferies has been a fisherman most of his life. He is shown here at Tunis Fishery, which he operated for a number of years with his brother, Walter.

Walter Jefferies, like his brother, Brantley, was a fisherman most of his life. Here he enjoys a cup of coffee in a boatload of herring at Tunis Fishery.

Opposite above: Walter and Brantley Jefferies and their Tunis Fishery pound net crew unload herring at the fishery. In one season of fishing for herring at Tunis Fishery, they caught over a million pounds of herring.

Opposite below: Brantley Jefferies uses a vacuum device to unload a boatload of herring at Tunis Fishery.

Leroy Eure lived and worked most of his life as a fisherman at Tunis on the Chowan River.

Victor Perry owned and operated Tunis Fishery for a number of years.

Myrna Elliott cleans and cuts herring at Tunis
Fishery.

Minnie Boone cut herring at Tunis Fishery for a
number of years.

Above: Two boatloads of herring waiting to be unloaded at Tunis Fishery in the mid-1980s.

Right: Victor Perry, who owned and operated Tunis Fishery for a number of years, repairs one of his pound nets.

In 1994 Tony Stephenson, who had been fishing commercially since 1978, acquired Tunis Fishery from Victor Perry and soon began remodeling the old fish house. This Tunis Fishery sign was made by Tony Stephenson and is located above the main entrance of the remodeled fish house.

Following his purchase of Tunis Fishery, Tony Stephenson and his crew remodeled the old fish house into what it is today.

Left to right: Shirley and Tony Stephenson, owners and operators of Tunis Fishery since 1994, are seen at the fishery with his sister, Kay Freehling from Garden Grove, California.

Left: Members of the Tunis Fishery pound net crew fish one of the fishery's pound nets on the Meherrin River.

Below: Tunis Fishery pound net crew members fish one of the fishery's pound nets on the Chowan River.

Tony Stephenson, owner and operator of Tunis Fishery, uses a hoist to dip herring from a pound net into his boat on the Chowan River.

Tunis Fishery pound netters fish on the Chowan River. Pound net fishing requires a rugged crew to handle the hard work involved.

Ken Mollett from Anaheim, California—a friend of Tony and Shirley Stephenson—experiences North Carolina herring fishing firsthand at Tunis Fishery. *Photograph by Tony Stephenson.*

Gene Jernigan, a member of the Tunis Fishery crew, brings in the hoist with another load of herring from one of the fishery's pound nets on the Chowan River.

Right: Mrs. Shirley Stephenson, chief cook at Tunis Fishery, cooks up another batch of mighty good eats to serve to the pound net crew after their early morning trip to fish on the Meherrin and Chowan Rivers.

Below: A hungry pound net crew enjoys Mrs. Shirley's mighty fine eats following their return from an early morning trip on the Meherrin and Chowan Rivers.

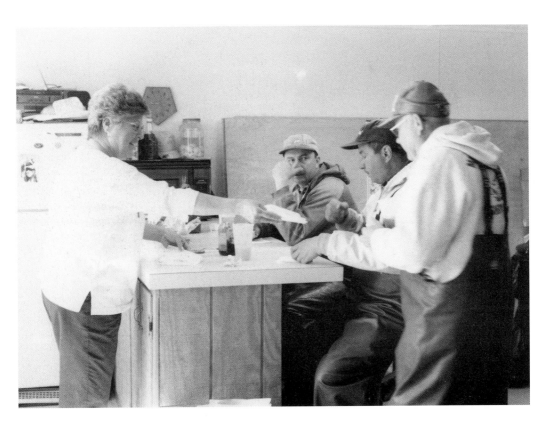

Tunis Fishery crew members Bobby Bryant, Lynn Harrell and Tony Stephenson clean fresh caught river herring for another customer.

Mrs. Shirley Stephenson and her father, C.M. Hoggard, enjoy a brief break at Tunis Fishery, where Mr. Hoggard is a member of the crew.

Ms. Connie DiPietro, niece of Tunis Fishery owner Tony Stephenson, is seen here as a member of the fishery's pound net crew and fishing one of the nets on the Chowan River.

Tunis Fishery pound net crew members, Olin Romines and his son, Dennis Romines, take a brief break before the next trip out to fish on the Chowan River.

Left: This is a pound net fishing crew at Tunis Fishery. Pictured from left to right are Troy Godwin, Lynn Harrell, Bobby Bryant, Shirley Stephenson, C.M. Hoggard, Tony Stephenson, Brenda Romines, Olin Romines and Justin Grizzard.

Below: This is another pound net fishing crew at Tunis Fishery. Pictured from left to right are Tony Stephenson, Lynn Harrell, Robert Pearson, Dennis Romines, Richard Knowles and Gene Jernigan.

David Hollowell Sr. was a longtime pound net fisherman on the Chowan River. He takes a break at Tunis Fishery where he and his son, David, fished for a number of years.

David Hollowell Jr. has fished pound nets on the Chowan River most of his life. Here he works on one of his pound nets at Tunis Fishery where he has fished for a number of years.

Terry Pratt from Merry Hill, North Carolina, has fished for river herring most of his life. Here he repairs a pound net at Tunis Fishery, from which he has fished on several occasions.

This Tunis Fishery employee pops open river herring to extract the roe, which is in high demand during the fishing season.

Tunis Fishery fishermen Tony Stephenson and Lynn Harrell roll herring into their boat from one of their Chowan River pound nets.

Fishery Book 1881—

This is the front cover of the 1881 sales book for the Petty Shore Seine Fishery—operated for a number of years on the Chowan River at Petty Shore by Colonel James M. Wynn of Murfreesboro. Petty Shore, a small fishing village south of Tunis, was home to a number of large herring haul seines down through the years.

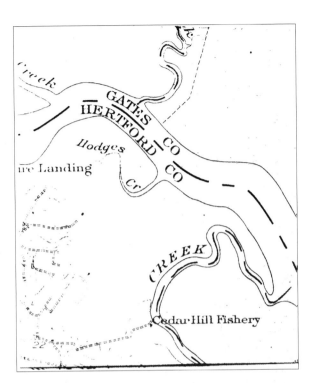

Right: Cedar Hill Fishery was a Hertford County herring haul seine that was located on the Wiccacon Creek, a tributary of the Chowan River. It was a very active herring haul seine—operating for many years in the 1800s and early 1900s—and is shown here on a 1909 Hertford County soil survey map. *Frank Stephenson Photo Archives.*

Below: This is a 1949 view of Swain's Mill Creek and the small fishing village that was actively involved in herring fishing on the Chowan River. *Courtesy North Carolina Department of Cultural Resources.*

Left: Another 1949 view of the herring fishing village that was located on Swain's Mill Creek in Hertford County. *Courtesy North Carolina Department of Cultural Resources.*

Below: One of the fish houses located on Swain's Mill Creek in Hertford County in 1949. *Courtesy North Carolina Department of Cultural Resources.*

Above: Sign for Hollowell's Fish Company that was located at Castelow's Landing on the Chowan River in Hertford County and was operated by Ed Hollowell.

Right: Ed Hollowell and his wife, Sandra, operated a pound net herring fishery at Castelow's Landing near Cofield for about twenty-five years.

Ed Hollowell operated Hollowell's Fish Company from this fish house on the Chowan River. Freshly caught river herring were processed in the fish house by a small crew of herring cutters.

Right: A member of the Hollowell Fish Company pound net crew unloads freshly caught herring.

Below: Herring cutters at Hollowell Fish Company, Cofield, North Carolina, process freshly caught river herring.

Herring cutters at Hollowell's Fish Company in Cofield, North Carolina.

Herring cutter processes newly caught river herring at Hollowell's Fish Company.

Herring cutter at Hollowell's Fish Company.

A herring cutter processes freshly caught river herring at Hollowell's Fish Company.

Terry Pratt's fish house at Shipyard Landing on
Cashote Creek in Bertie County.

Terry Pratt and a friend clean freshly caught river
herring at his fish house at Shipyard Landing on
Cashote Creek in Bertie County.

Herring fish house at Shipyard Landing on Cashote Creek in Bertie County.

Herring fish houses hug the shore of Cashote Creek at Shipyard Landing in Bertie County.

Spanish moss and herring fish houses at Shipyard Landing on Cashote Creek in Bertie County.

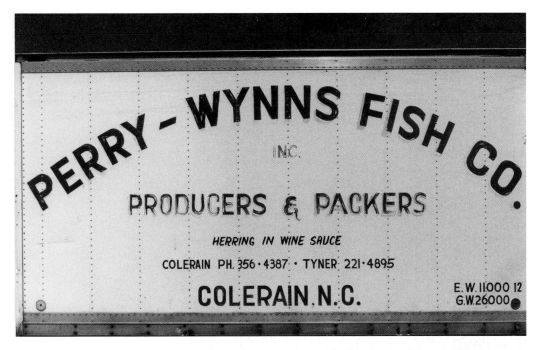

Perry-Wynns Fish Company, located in Colerain, North Carolina, was the world's largest herring processing plant until it was destroyed by Hurricane Isabelle in 2003.

The Colerain town tag proudly displays the citation for the largest herring fishery.

Southern view of Perry-Wynns Fish Company.

Northern view of Perry-Wynns Fish Company.

Opposite: Undated advertisement for Perry-Wynns Fish Company, Colerain, North Carolina. *Frank Stephenson Photo Archives*.

Waterfront view of Perry-Wynns Fish Company.

1949 view of Perry-Wynns Fish Company. *Courtesy North Carolina Department of Cultural Resources.*

Above: Mike Perry was one of the co-owners and operators of Perry-Wynns Fish Company.

Right: Lee Wynns was another of the co-owners and operators of Perry-Wynns Fish Company.

Lennie Perry was one of the owners and
operators of Perry-Wynns Fish Company.

Norman Perry, Perry-Wynns Fish Company.

One of the metal tins that Perry-Wynns
Fish Company used to market Tidewater
Brand salt herring.

One of the metal tins used by Perry-Wynns to market
salt herring.

Above and right: Herring boats unload freshly caught river herring at Perry-Wynns Fish Company.

Right: Two fully loaded herring boats unload at Perry-Wynns Fish Company. *Courtesy Perry-Wynns Fish Company.*

Below: In the early morning, sunlight herring boats unload freshly caught river herring at Perry-Wynns Fish Company.

Herring cutters process newly caught fresh herring at Perry-Wynns Fish Company.

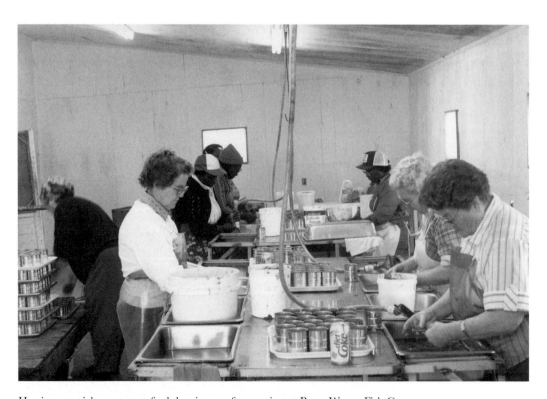

Herring roe pickers prepare fresh herring roe for canning at Perry-Wynns Fish Company.

Above: Huge vats of newly cut fresh river herring are salted at Perry-Wynns Fish Company. *Courtesy Perry-Wynns Fish Company.*

Right: Mr. Leo Wynns, chief executive officer at Perry-Wynns Fish Company, examines a vat of salted herring. *Courtesy Perry-Wynns Fish Company.*

Above: Vats of salted fresh herring cure at Perry-Wynns Fish Company. *Courtesy Perry-Wynns Fish Company.*

Opposite below: Employees of Perry-Wynns Fish Company install headers in barrels of salted herring. *Courtesy Perry-Wynns Fish Company.*

Today's N. C Poem

THE BEAUTIFUL

I knew them once in pauper rags,
So humble their apparel,
Their ghettos were as artless as
The rusting of a barrel,
But now they pose in royal wrap,
To appetites, quite stirring,
"Move over, steak, you have a
    guest,
The beautiful salt herring."

PAULINE WIGGINS

Seaboard

Above: This undated poem—penned by Mrs. Pauline Wiggins of Seaboard, North Carolina—appeared in an issue of the *Roanoke-Chowan News-Herald*, Ahoskie, North Carolina. *Frank Stephenson Photo Archives.*

In December 1968, the two top executive officers of Perry-Wynns Fish Company, Mr. Leo Wynns and Mr. Lennie Perry, celebrate the end of the fall packing season by cutting a cake. *Courtesy Perry-Wynns Fish Company.*

These metal advertising signs were attached to the sides of Perry-Wynns Fish Company delivery trucks.

Chowan River fishermen found this 180-pound sturgeon in their pound nets on the morning of April 15, 1977, and brought it to Perry-Wynns Fish Company. The fish measured seven feet and one inch. Once in awhile one of these big fish is caught during herring season. The fishermen who caught the big fish are (from left) Elton Bunch, Percy Bass and Marcus Bass. In the background is Willie Bunch. *Courtesy the* Roanoke-Chowan News-Herald.

131

Perry-Wynns Fish Company's Seagull Café is a very popular place to eat during herring season. In herring season, the menu consists of fried fresh herring, white perch and herring roe. Hundreds of patrons come from near, far and wide to enjoy some mighty fine eating. In fact, during the 2006 herring season, two patrons dropped in by helicopter. Salt herring, shrimp and oysters are on the menu when the Seagull Café is open in the fall.

Advertisement for the spring herring season at the Seagull Café at Perry-Wynns Fish Company in Colerain, North Carolina. The advertisement is from the February 14, 2006 issue of the *Roanoke-Chowan News-Herald*, Ahoskie, North Carolina.

The Byrum family of Chowan County has operated a herring fishery at Cannon's Ferry on the Chowan River for many years.

Byrum's Fishery is located on the Chowan River at Cannon's Ferry and is operated seasonally by Herbert and Bobby Byrum.

Herbert Byrum, along with his brother, Bobby, has been fishing for herring most of his life. Herbert and Bobby Byrum are following in the footsteps of four earlier generations of Byrum men who were herring fishermen on the Chowan River.

Bobby Byrum, like his brother Herbert, has fished the Chowan River for herring for most of his life.

Mr. Jimmy Byrum, father of Herbert and Bobby Byrum, was a lifelong herring fisherman and worked with his sons at Byrum's Fishery at Cannon's Ferry in Chowan County.

Mrs. Carrie Byrum, wife of Mr. Jimmy Byrum, was an active member of the Byrum Brothers herring fishing crew at Byrum's Fishery at Cannon's Ferry.

Mrs. Betty Byrum, wife of Herbert Byrum, has worked for over forty years in herring fishing with her husband and his brother, Bobby.

Left: This quiet and tranquil scene at Byrum's Fishery at Cannon's Ferry reflects the natural beauty of the Chowan River.

Opposite above: The small fishing village at Cannon's Ferry was home to a duke's mixture of fish houses and herring processing facilities. Millions and millions of river herring were landed and processed here. The two-story white building was a herring processing facility operated by Perry-Wynns Fish Company.

Opposite below: These hoppers at Cannon's Ferry were used to load freshly caught river herring in tractor-trailers and dump trucks for transport to market.

Ed. Ward's fish house was one of several fish houses located at Cannon's Ferry.

This is a 1964 view of Perry-Wynns Fish Company's roe canning plant (left) and fish meal facility that was located at Cannon's Ferry. There was a refrigeration facility in this same complex of buildings. For about five years in the late 1940s and early 1950s, the Perry-Belch-Wynn Fish Company, forerunner of Perry-Wynns Fish Company, operated a herring processing facility on the Connecticut River at Middletown, Connecticut. This facility was necessary because during that time period, herring catches in the Chowan River were low and the company sought an alternate source of herring. *Photograph by Roy Johnson.*

Above: This is Elbert and Robert Nixon's Herring Fishery, located at Rocky Hock Landing on the Chowan River.

Right: Mr. Elbert Nixon was an avid and lifelong Chowan River fisherman. He operated a small herring fishery at Rocky Hock Landing on the Chowan River.

Peele's Herring Fishery was located at Rocky Hock Landing on the Chowan River.

Mr. Wallace Peele, along with brothers J.D. and Lloyd and nephew Carroll, operated Peele's Herring Fishery located at Rocky Hock Landing on the Chowan River.

Above: This is Peele's Herring Fishery, located at Rocky Hock Landing and operated by three Peele Brothers and nephew Carroll Peele.

Right: Mr. J.D. Peele was one of three brothers who operated Peele's Herring Fishery at Rocky Hock Landing.

This is an old herring processing facility at White's Landing on the Chowan River. There were several fish houses at White's Landing.

There were a number of herring fish houses located on the Chowan River at Harris Landing or Tynch Town. Will Tynch, Spurgeon Tynch, Murray Tynch, Stanley Tynch, Carroll Tynch, Milton Tynch, Mike Tynch and Ricky Tynch were some of the men who fished for herring out of Tynch Town or Harris Landing.

Murray Nixon Fishery is located on Nixon Fishery Road on Route 2 in Edenton, North Carolina.

Murray Nixon Fishery was founded by Murray L. Nixon, who first started selling herring in toe sacks out of the back of a pickup truck. Today Murray Nixon Fishery ships seafood all over the United States.

Murray L. Nixon, founder of Murray Nixon's Fishery, Route 2, Edenton, North Carolina.

Right: Ricky Nixon, son of Murray Nixon, has worked in commercial fishing all of his life. Today Ricky is co-owner of Murray Nixon's Fishery and co-owner and manager of Nixon's Family Restaurant at 327 River Road, Edenton, North Carolina.

Below: Leon Nixon, son of Murray Nixon, washes and scales fresh caught river herring at Murray Nixon Fishery, Route 2, Edenton, North Carolina. Today Leon operates Leon Nixon's Catering near Edenton. At one time, Ricky and Leon Nixon's brothers, Louis and Jimmy, worked in herring fishing. Today Louis is farming and Jimmy is in construction.

In this 1960s photo, Murray Nixon fishes one of his baskets on the Chowan River. *Courtesy Murray L. Nixon.*

The remains of a fish meal plant that the Woff brothers operated on the Chowan River near Edenton.

Chapter Four

HERRING DIPPING AND MORE

Dipping for herring in Eastern North Carolina is more fun than you can shake a fish at! In the spring, when the herring begin to arrive in large numbers in Eastern North Carolina streams to spawn, residents grab whatever they can find to use as a dipping device and head to the local creek or river to dip up a mess of fresh river herring. Some herring dipping devices include hand-held dip nets, hand-held seine, cast nets, wire baskets, wire basket-like devices, an umbrella-shaped net, skimmers and anything else that can be used to scoop up river herring. Some herring dippers have been known to use discarded plastic laundry baskets, old tubs, buckets, shallow pans and even old straw hats to dip up herring. When the herring are thick in numbers and flopping against the shore, some folks have been known to use their hands to catch herring and toss them up on the bank. The hand-held bow net, though, is by far the most popular device utilized by herring dippers in Eastern North Carolina.

A herring bow is an odd-looking thing that resembles a figure eight. A baggy net hangs from an enlarged end and a smaller, sawed-off end serves as a handle. Most herring bows are made from two small debarked cedar trees ten to fifteen feet in length. If the trees were not debarked, the netting would get caught on the bark. Cedar is the wood of choice for making herring bows because it is more flexible and rot-resistant than other types of wood. Most makers of herring bow nets use some kind of homemade device to force the two cedar trees permanently into the shape of a bow as it seasons. When the shaped herring bow is removed from its forming device, the netting is carefully installed so that it hangs and bags just right so the fish that are caught in it do not fall out before they are landed. Netting that is properly installed bags with the current and allows the bow net fisherman to hold a small piece of the netting with one finger while waiting for a slight tug on the net that signals the user to lift and empty his catch of fish.

A large number of herring bow net fishermen made their own bow nets, but through the years there have been a number of commercial bow net makers in Eastern North Carolina. Perhaps one of the more prolific and outstanding bow net makers is Johnny Shelton of Garysburg in Northampton County, who has hand crafted twenty-five bow nets or more each year for over forty-five years in a workshop in his backyard. Johnny Shelton makes herring bows in all sizes, including smaller ones for women and children. While Johnny Shelton's bow nets have enjoyed wide distribution, two of his more popular outlets were Planters Hardware and the Sports Mart in Murfreesboro.

Probably one of the best places to see one of Johnny Shelton's finished products in action is at Vaughan's Creek, just north of Murfreesboro on the Hertford and Northampton County line. Vaughan's Creek is one of the premier herring bow netting spots in Eastern North Carolina. People from far and wide come in droves to dip for herring at Vaughan's Creek. At the height of the herring fishing season, it is nearly impossible to drive through the Vaughan's Creek area; vehicles bearing license tags from all around North Carolina and Virginia line the roadways. In fact, it is not uncommon to find one hundred or more fishermen with old washtubs tethered to them standing chest-deep in Vaughan's Creek using Johnny Shelton's bow nets. These fishermen will remain chest-deep in Vaughan's Creek's juniper-colored water for hours—or until someone upstream hollers, "Snake heading your way!"

Most of the herring caught at Vaughan's Creek was carried home for consumption within one or two days. Large numbers of herring were carried home and salted down for use during the upcoming fall and winter months. Each spring, during the herring season, my father would salt down four or five hundred herring for family use—particularly in case there was a bad crop year. Salt herring—along with sweet potatoes, collards and corn bread—is a popular dish in Eastern North Carolina. Some herring caught at Vaughan's Creek were sold right there to buyers and to civic organizations for use in fundraiser dinners. Some of the herring caught at Vaughan's Creek were cooked and consumed right on the creek bank. The unmistakable aroma of fresh fried herring filtering through the cypress and juniper trees at Vaughan's Creek is enough to cause a herring bow net fisherman to temporarily put down his bow in search of some mighty good eating.

Today, at seventy-three years young, Johnny Shelton, the Bow Net Man, is still making bow nets with great care in the workshop in his backyard off North Carolina Highway 186 between Gumberry and Garysburg, North Carolina. He is one of the last craftsmen in North Carolina practicing the lost art of making handcrafted herring bows as if each were his own.

The Vaughan's Creek herring fishing scenes described above have been repeated thousands of times over through the years in the spring at numerous creeks and rivers across Eastern North Carolina, where river herring return each year to spawn. One of the more popular questions asked in the springtime in Eastern North Carolina is not "Will you marry me?" but rather, "Got any herrings?" What a poignant question it is now, with the statewide ban on herring fishing imposed by the Marine Fisheries Commission in effect in North Carolina for 2007—and perhaps for many years to come.

Mrs. Gurney Eure and Mrs. Linwood Askew enjoy a fresh herring cookout in the early 1940s at Ray's Beach on the Chowan River in Gates County. The old Ray's Beach fish house can be seen in the background. *Courtesy Mrs. D.L Eure, Eure, North Carolina.*

Bud Eure of Eure, North Carolina, has fished on the Chowan River for many years. He comes from an old Gates County herring fishing family and for the past four years he has fished pound nets for herring off Ray's Beach.

Left: Johnny Shelton of Garysburg, North Carolina acquired the name "Bow Net Man" for a good reason. Shelton has made hundreds of herring bow nets through the years. Johnny Shelton's bow nets have been very popular with herring fishermen at Vaughan's Creek north of Murfreesboro.

Below: Johnny Shelton used this sign to advertise his bow nets. The sign stood in front of his bow net shop on North Carolina Highway 186 near Garysburg, North Carolina.

Ernest Britt, a herring bow net fisherman from Conway, North Carolina, checks out the scene at Vaughan's Creek, a favorite herring fishing location on the Northampton–Hertford County line north of Murfreesboro.

Hillary Davis, a herring bow net fisherman from Conway, North Carolina, repairs his bow net for another visit to Vaughan's Creek north of Murfreesboro. Mr. Davis fished for herring at Vaughan's Creek most of his life and he took his grandson, Quinton Jenkins, with him on numerous trips. *Courtesy Mr. and Mrs. Quinton Jenkins, Como, North Carolina.*

Vaughan's Creek has been a favorite spot for herring bow net fishermen for years.

A herring bow net fisherman at Vaughan's Creek checks his bow net.

Above: A herring bow net fisherman takes a break on the banks of Vaughan's Creek. During the herring fishing season, this creek attracts fishermen from miles around.

Right: A herring bow net fisherman dumps his catch of river herring at Vaughan's Creek.

Left: Herring fishermen use all types of devices at Vaughan's Creek. Here a herring fisherman uses an umbrella-shaped net.

Below: This Vaughan's Creek herring fisherman uses a wire basket-like device to fish for river herring.

Right: This sign advertised the availability of fresh herring at the Family Mart in Como, North Carolina, operated by Mr. and Mrs. Louis Gore. The Family Mart had a small eatery and Mrs. Gore sure could cook up some mighty tasty fried fresh herring dinners.

Below: One of the best ways to enjoy fresh river herring is to cook and eat it right on the creek bank, In this photo, a group of men enjoy fried fresh herring on the banks of Vaughan's Creek.

Left: This crock was used by the Ross Nichols Family of the Earlys Station community in Hertford County to salt herring for year-round use. *Courtesy Mrs. Barbara Nichols Mulder.*

Below: The Perrytown Volunteer Fire Department in Bertie County held its forty-third annual salt herring dinner fundraiser on November 17, 2006. The ad appeared in the November 3, 2006 issue of the *Roanoke-Chowan News-Herald*, Ahoskie, North Carolina.

Opposite above: Corned or salted herring dinners were used by numerous civic clubs and organizations as fundraisers—as seen in this advertisement for the St. John Fire Department in Hertford County. The ad appeared in the January 24, 1994 issue of the *Roanoke-Chowan News-Herald* of Ahoskie, North Carolina.

43rd ANNUAL
Herring Supper
Friday, November 17, 2006
4:00 p.m. till 8:00 p.m.
PERRYTOWN COMMUNITY BUILDING
$6.00 Per Plate
EAT IN *or* TAKE OUT

SPONSORED BY:
Perrytown Volunteer Fire Department

ALL PROCEEDS BENEFIT THE
PERRYTOWN VOLUNTEER FIRE DEPARTMENT

Thank You For Your Support!

St. John Fire Dept. sets corned herring supper

ST. JOHN — The St. John Fire Department will hold a corned herring supper from 4-8 p.m. Jan. 26 at the fire department.

Plates will be $5, which includes eat-in or take-out plates.

In the 1940s and 1950s—during the glory days of moonshine operations in Eastern North Carolina—there were several occasions when bootleggers and pound net fishermen crossed paths on the Chowan River. In the 1950s in Hertford County, a large still shipped its moonshine by boat using a small canal to access the Chowan River and points north. In this particular case, on a fog-shrouded Chowan River, the bootleggers were not aware that pound net fishermen fish very early in the morning. A boat full of moonshine collided with a boat full of herring—sinking both. A second boat of pound netters was nearby and picked up both crews and all parties reached an amiable and quiet settlement off the record. *Frank Stephenson Photo Archives.*

Corned or salted herring remain a popular dinner in Eastern North Carolina. This ad for corned herring dinners at the Golden Skillet in Ahoskie, North Carolina appeared in the July 8, 1995 issue of the *Roanoke-Chowan News-Herald*, Ahoskie, North Carolina.

Left: A number of Gates County fishermen used Pipkin Landing to fish their pound nets on the Chowan River. *1964 photograph by Roy Johnson.*

Opposite above: Cypress Grill, located in Jamesville, North Carolina, has been operated for thirty-five years by Leslie and Sally Gardner. Perhaps the most famous herring eatery in North Carolina, it is the focal point for Jamesville's annual Easter Monday Herring Festival, which attracts several thousand herring lovers to the banks of the Roanoke River for the chance to eat fried fresh river herring. Other prominent herring eateries in Eastern North Carolina are the Seagull Café at Colerain and the Filling Station restaurant in Robersonville.

CATFISH MUDDLE
Annual Como Ruritan Club Auction Sale
Friday, March 11, 1994
Serving Meal - 5:00 P.M. to 6:30 P.M.
$4.00 per plate or $6.00 per quart
Auction Sale Begins at 6:30 P.M.
To be held at Como Community Building
Turn off U.S. 258 onto State Road 1317
Go 1/4 mile & building is on your left

A catfish or rockfish muddle is also a popular fundraiser for Eastern North Carolina civic organization, as seen in this March 11, 1994 ad for the Como, North Carolina Ruritan Club. The muddle consists of fish, country bacon, onions, eggs, crackers, butter and red pepper all mixed together in an old iron washpot. A properly cooked fish muddle can be eaten with a fork. If the cooked fish muddle requires a spoon to eat it, then it is more like a fish stew—and good fish muddle is not fish stew! *Frank Stephenson Photo Archives.*

Left: Tyler Edwards Herring Seine Fishery was located on the Nottoway River near Franklin, Virginia. It was started in the late 1920s by Tyler Edwards Sr. and Clyde Edwards. The seine was operated into the 1970s by John Moody. The herring caught in Virginia on the Blackwater, Nottoway and Meherrin Rivers have migrated through the Chowan River in North Carolina and finally into Virginia. *Photo courtesy Southampton Historical Society, Courtland, Virginia.*

Below: The Cotton Family herring seine was also located on the Nottoway River near Franklin, Virginia. Every Easter Monday the Cotton Family would gather at the seine fishery to enjoy fried fresh herring, potatoes, slaw and corn bread. *Photo courtesy Mrs. Valentine Cotton, Woodland, North Carolina.*